THE RESONANT MALE SINGER

Daily Vocal Workouts to Encourage Young Men

★ BY JACOB NARVERUD ★

SHAWNEE PRESS

ISBN-13: 978-1-49505-024-4

Published by Hal Leonard Corporation
7777 W. Bluemound Road
P.O. Box 13819
Milwaukee, WI 53213

Library of Congress Cataloging-in-Publication Data

Names: Narverud, Jacob J., author.
Title: The resonant male singer : daily vocal workouts to engage and empower
   young men / by Jacob Narverud.
Description: Milwaukee, Wisconsin : Shawnee Press, 2016.
Identifiers: LCCN 2015050230 I ISBN 9781495050244 (pbk.)
Subjects: LCSH: Singing--Studies and exercises. I Singing--Instruction and
   study. I Voice culture.
Classification: LCC MT885 .N37 2016 I DDC 783.8/144--dc23
LC record available at http://lccn.loc.gov/2015050230

Printed in the U.S.A.
First Edition

In Australia Contact:
Hal Leonard Australia Pty. Ltd.
4 Lentara Court
Cheltenham, Victoria, 3192 Australia
Email: ausadmin@halleonard.com.au

Visit Hal Leonard Online at www.halleonard.com
Visit Shawnee Press Online at www.shawneepress.com

TABLE OF CONTENTS

EXCLUSIVELY DISTRIBUTED BY

HAL•LEONARD®
CORPORATION

7777 W. BLUEMOUND RD. P.O. BOX 13819 MILWAUKEE, WI 53213

Visit Shawnee Press Online at
www.shawneepress.com

Visit Hal Leonard Online at
www.halleonard.com

Special Thanks

To the teachers, mentors, friends, and family who have made an impact in my life:

Terry Barham, Cory Ganschow, Ed diZerega, Robert Bode, Christy Elsner, Janeal Krehbiel, Charles Bruffy, Judith Clurman, Hilary Morton, Gretchen Harrison, Carolyn Welch, Ken Prewitt, Stanford Felix, Penelope Speedie, Gary Ziek, Vernon Yenne, Jo-Michael Scheibe, Eugene Butler, Sheree Stoppel, Anthony Edwards, Sarah Tyrrell, Katie Grose, Lori Egan, David Narverud, Vivian Narverud, Austin Narverud, Amanda Narverud, Joshua East.

To the singers pictured in this book:

Stephen Holbert, Ben Heigele, Simon Stewart, Zac Matthew, Jacob DeSett, Allen Weinert, Porter Hacking, Zach Hoeven, Jack Torline.

Introduction

So, you've been given the challenging task, yet incredible privilege, of working with young male singers. Now, where to begin? A favorite professor of mine once had a sign on his office door that read, "Start Anywhere." And "anywhere" is a great place to start, indeed!

It is a common misconception that when middle and high school male voices are changing it is not possible for them to produce a rich, masculine tone. False! In fact, now is the perfect time to teach your students how to develop a vibrant, healthy, and mature sound through proper vocal technique and training.

What are some benefits of teaching resonant singing?

1. Your singers will get a better tone, one that is free and exciting. If the sound is focused at the hard palate, the sound will be crisp, bright, and vibrant. If the sound is caught in the back of the throat, the sound will be dull, dark, and muffled.

2. Your singers will be able to manage their breath more easily. It takes much less breath to make sound if your voice is vibrating off a hard surface (hard palate) than if in the back of your throat (soft palate).

3. Your singers will dramatically increase their vocal power and projection (15 singers can sound like 50 or more when singing with proper resonance and intensity).

4. Your singers will sound and feel like MEN instead of BOYS!

How to Use This Book

Consider yourself the "coach" or "personal trainer" for your young men as they develop their voices each day in your choir. The "workouts" offered in this book are intended to help guide you along this vocal journey with your singers. The information here is not new, by any means. Rather, it is collected, compiled, and developed ideas on how to teach resonance in ways that young men can understand, relate, and respond to. I've been fortunate to work with some inspiring mentors and colleagues who have helped to shape my philosophy on choral tone and imagery. In this book I will share what has worked for me with male voices, from seventh grade boys through college men and beyond.

Pick your favorite exercises and try a few each day. Rotate them to keep the rehearsals fresh and exciting. The high expectations and positive attitude you create for your young men at the beginning of this process will ultimately determine where they arrive.

Tip:

STAND. ALL THE TIME. There's no need to sit unless you are giving markings for music. Our bodies are not designed to sit while singing. Most people sit for hours on end during the day. Choir rehearsal is a time to activate the mind, body, and spirit!

CHAPTER 1:
Body, Breath, & Energy

The first step to healthy, resonant, vocal production is to engage the breath, and the quickest way to do so is by moving the body. We can help our singers develop healthy rehearsal habits by teaching them to sing with internal and external energy at all times. The exercises in this chapter are designed to do just that.

DO first, EXPLAIN later (show before you tell)

The philosophy above applies to everything in this book. Say to your singers, "Do what I do." Just show them without talking. They will imitate. We all began imitating at birth, so it comes naturally. Also, allow plenty of room between each singer for these exercises. Each person should have an "imaginary friend" between him and the person closest to him.

- **SUN BREATH -** Make a circle with your arms over your head and stretch! Take a "sun breath" by inhaling and exhaling through your nose. Since your arms are over your head, it is not possible to move your chest—this allows you to feel that the breath is low in the body.

- **SHAKE IT OFF -** Shake your wrists and hands at your side vigorously as if trying to get water off of them. Try shaking at different speeds, then shake only your fingertips.

- **SHOULDER ROLL -** Roll your shoulders back, then forward, then one at a time, then one forward and one backward at the same time.

- **ARM STRETCH –** Look up to the ceiling and reach up to the sky with both arms, then left arm, then right arm. Remind your singers to breathe during this exercise (they will want to hold their breath).

- **WASHING MACHINE -** With your feet together, stretch your legs and torso and make fists with your hands. Twist your arms and body from side to side, imitating the movement inside of a washing machine. Try a fast cycle, then a slow cycle.

- **HEAD ROLL -** Gently and very slowly roll your head from side to side while standing tall with your feet centered shoulder-width apart.
- **ARM CIRCLES -** Reach your arms out and make circles that are big, then small.
- **SHOULDER SHRUG -** Shrug your shoulders up, then down, then up, then down, then up (hold), then down. Try this at different speeds.
- **FIELD GOAL -** Stand strong, proud and tall in "prayer position." Be sure to keep your chest raised. Pull your hands apart to create a "field goal," and then lower your arms to side while the chest remains "puffed", creating excellent posture.

Tip:
Time is precious. Don't waste a second in rehearsals. Be efficient and keep things moving! The singers should not have time to think about anything but the task at hand.

- **PANT LIKE A DOG -** Place one hand low on your stomach, then stick out your tongue and pant like a dog on a hot day. Feel that your breath is activated low in your diaphragm, just above the belt.
- **HISS LIKE A CAT -** Put your hands up and claws out. Inhale and "hiss" like a cat, three times staccato at the front of the face.

Achh

- **ACHH -** Cross your arms in front of you in an "X." Make an "achh" sound in the back of your throat, three times staccato.

- **STIR THE POT -** Place one hand out as if you are holding the bottom of a large cooking pot, then stir the pot of spaghetti with the other hand. Stir the pot quickly while you are buzzing your lips. This gives the sensation of stirring ("spinning") the air inside the body.

- **SUPER HERO MOVING A BUS -** Press forward with both hands like a super hero moving a bus. Feel the resistance and momentum to create body awareness and the feeling of tension in the neck and upper torso, which should all be released when singing. After moving the bus, "shake it off" to release all tension.

- **RAISE THE ROOF -** Press upward with both hands like you are raising the roof off a house. Feel the resistance and momentum as in the previous exercise, then release all tension.

Raise the Roof

- **EYEBROW PUSHUPS** - Smile (with teeth), place index fingers on each eyebrow and physically move the eyebrows with your fingers up and down 10 times. This allows the singers to be aware of the difference between when the brows are lifted and when they are not. Why is this important? If there is no "lift" in the upper portion of the face when singing, proper resonance cannot occur.

- **THE SCREAM** - Place your hands on either side of your face, open your mouth and eyes wide, and pretend to scream (without making any noise). Ask the students to lower their hands along their cheeks and feel how low their jaw can drop, then say "Ah ha!" as though you have just discovered something new and wonderful.

Tip:

Keep your singers moving constantly—singing is athletic and involves the entire body! Be aggressive and passionate—energy is contagious!

- **NEANDERTHAL EYES** - Have your students place their index finger across their eyebrows and imitate the face of a Neanderthal (no emotion, lack of interest, etc.)

Next, ask your students to be a modern human again—gently massage and "tickle" the areas above the eyebrows and at the cheeks to create body awareness and the importance of keeping the eyes open and brows lifted.

Neanderthal Eyes

Tip:

Productive rehearsals require active thought and discipline. Train the singers to do certain things which cause immediate reactions. Director: "Shh, shh, shh" Singers: "Shh, shh, shh"(silence).

CHAPTER 2:
Muscles and Movement

As singers, much of what we do involves more than just producing a good tone. We are responsible for telling a story to our audience with every musical work we perform. We become an "actor" and are alive in the moment and in the story. This does not happen naturally. We must work on facial expressions on a daily basis. The exercises in this chapter are similar to those in Chapter One but are geared more toward body awareness and visual communication skills through the use of various muscles and body movement.

- **BOULDER TOSS** - Crouch down and pick up a giant boulder, then raise it slowly while standing upright and toss the boulder behind your head, all while singing a siren from lowest to highest note and back down. Remind your singers to lift with their legs and not with their backs!

- **GRUMPY vs. HAPPY** - Shrink your body in as small as possible. Scrunch your hands near your face and give a "grumpy Monday-morning" face.

Then open-up "Big face, little body!"

Scrunch in again. Ask singers to tense up all of their muscles.

Then open up with a million dollar face. "Big face, big body!" Release all tension!

Tip:
Share stories, experiences, and life lessons with one another during rehearsal. It creates trust and vulnerability, which ultimately leads to genuine music-making.

7

- **SOLDIER/SUMO** - Show your singers how to stand like a British soldier guarding the Queen: arms at your side, feet together, stern look on your face. No talking, no movement. This creates extreme focus and silence. Then have them hold the pose, count to three slowly, and then instantly become a sumo wrestler! Take a sumo position (crouch down, arms out) and grunt "HUH!" loud and low in the voice. Repeat a couple of times, then relax. This creates group discipline and body awareness.

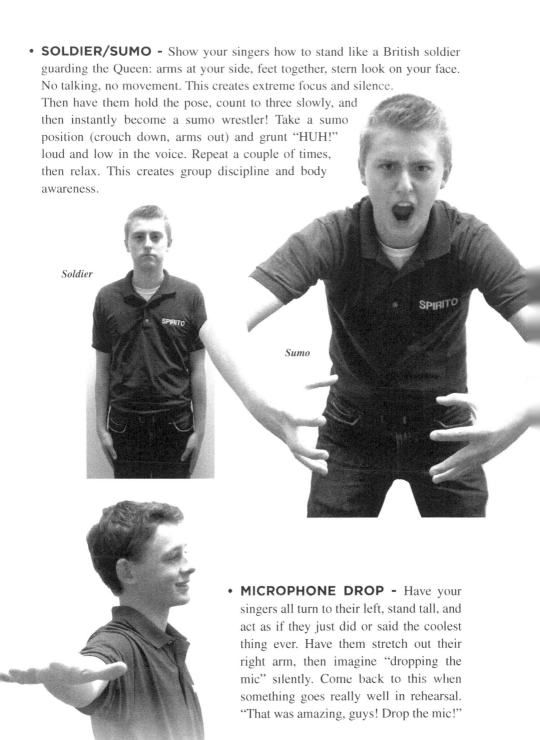

Soldier

Sumo

- **MICROPHONE DROP** - Have your singers all turn to their left, stand tall, and act as if they just did or said the coolest thing ever. Have them stretch out their right arm, then imagine "dropping the mic" silently. Come back to this when something goes really well in rehearsal. "That was amazing, guys! Drop the mic!"

- **TWO TOADS -** Ask your students to repeat after you. Speak the poem below, line by line, with a silly British accent. Create a physical movement for each line. Focus on good articulation and diction, proper text stress, intense energy, and tall classic vowels. After the exercise, ask students to raise their hands and describe the purpose of this activity—what is it reminding us to do as singers/ musicians?

Two toads, (students repeat with same energy and movement)
terribly tired, ("terribly tired")
trotted along the road. (cont.)
Said toad number one
to toad number two,
"It's hot and I carry a load!"
Said toad number two
to toad number one,
"Why don't we return to the pond?"
Said toad number one
to toad number two,
"That's a splendid idea!
Of walking I've never been fond."
So...
they turned in their tracks
and they scurried away,
not wasting a moment of time.
And back at the pond
for the rest of the day
they wallowed in ooze and in slime!

Tip:
Find students who are doing things well and have them demonstrate for the choir. Have the choir clap for that student once they have demonstrated also. This helps to develop camaraderie and good sportsmanship among the ensemble.

CHAPTER 3:
Exploring the Voice

It is important for young men to explore their voices and the sounds they are able to make. Guys must feel completely comfortable in all areas of their range before they will sing with confidence. Moan, grunt, holler, and make some noise! Once they hear how much sound they can make as a group, they will not want to hear anything less.

TYPES OF SOUND

Explore all types of sounds in rehearsal. The voice is the most versatile instrument! Sing nasal, sing "woofy." Create as many sounds together as possible to show the many possibilities:

- **VOICE FALL -** Demonstrate, try, then explain the natural "break" or "crack" in the voice. Some singers may not have a break at all and may be able to "travel" smoothly from one register to another. Use your arm (high to low) to create a visualization of the voice "falling."

- **GREETINGS -** Say "Hi!" in a resonant, "radio announcer" voice and wave to one another across the room. Show your grin!

- **FRAT GUY -** Be a preppy frat guy and say "yah brah!" (Yeah Bro). Since there is no tension, this releases the jaw and makes a great "ah" vowel.

- **DAH! -** Speak "dah dah dah" annoyingly bright and as close to the front teeth as possible.

Ha!

- **LAWN MOWER -** Imitate the sound of a (resonant) lawn mower as it passes by a window outside (Rrrrrrreeerrreerrrr).

- **AH HA! -** Say "Ah Ha!" as though you just remembered something exciting and important, with your tongue down at the front of the teeth. Place your index fingers on either side of the nostrils, on the cheekbones, and press upwards to create the space. If the singers start to yawn, don't take it personally—that means they are doing it correctly! Tell them that is where the proper space is that we need when singing.

SPIRITO

- **UP AND OVER** - Toss a baseball "up and over" and exclaim "Yah!" Encourage the singers to follow through with the throw and to fall through their range while coming down (play with the different sounds—bright, dark, swallowed—and imitate how the throw would look to match that same sound).

- **FREE THROW/WAITER-** Pantomime making a "free throw" basketball shot while lightly exclaiming "Wow!" Explain to your singers that the arch of the hand is the same arch that should occur on the roof of your mouth when singing, approaching each note from above. Now hold the same free throw arm out next to your body but this time pretend as though you are a waiter carrying a tray of food. Now say "Wow" in a deadbeat, boring manner with no arch or lift in the mouth, approaching from below. Explain to your singers that this is the wrong way to sing. Then shoot another free throw and say "Wow!" with even more excitement and arch!

- **TARZAN YELL** - Perform a "Tarzan" yell and chest thump. Practice the register break from chest voice to falsetto.

- **THE HOOK** - Have your singers imitate a pirate hook and place it below their nose. Then say "ARRRRRR" while moving your hook out beyond your eyes. The "ARRRR" should be focused at the nose. Ask them to see how much resonance they can activate, then change to "Ah!!" while keeping the hook up and moving it forward out in front of their eyes.

The Hook

HEAD VOICE EXERCISES

It is important for young men to sing in their head voice and falsetto registers on a daily basis as their voices are changing. This is how they develop comfort and ease throughout their range and also how true tenors are "born." Explain to your singers that the head voice is a mixture of the chest voice and falsetto. The "ease" in this voice can be developed through the daily workouts below.

- **SIRENS** – Practice making siren sounds in the head voice. Say "Hello!"

- **WATER LIFT** – On a warm, pure "Noo" vowel, have the singers act as though they are lifting a pan of water in front of them. Have them bend the knees and lift upward. Encourage the guys to keep the voice light as they descend through their passagio or "break." Smooth out the sound by changing to "Nee" ("Ee" vowel with "Oo" lips), then into "Ah" as they get into the meatier part of their voices. The sound should never feel pressed, but rather "lifted."

- **PUPPY DOG** - To find resonance in the head voice, massage the temples and make puppy dog whines and noises (be sure the sound is "heady" and not caught in the throat). Descend on "Moi" and keep the sound in the same location as the puppy dog whines (at the temples).

- **YOU KNOW ME WELL** - Work through the awkward chest and head voice area by singing pure vowels of "You Know Me Well" through the "sleeve of sound." Like the sleeve of a shirt, keep all vowels properly aligned through the tunnel of the sleeve. With all voices in unison, begin by breathing in the vowel of the first word "Oo" and keeping the vowel tall and aligned. Try removing the consonants and singing only on the vowels.

Also, be careful on the descending "me well." The singers will want to switch into to their full chest voice, which may result in voice cracking. Encourage

12

your guys to "lighten up" and stay in their head voice as they come down. Practice shadow vowels on beat two (Wel-lih). Add some movement (raise a pointer finger up to the air as you descend).

You know me__ well. You know me__ well. You

- **TOOEE -** Have your students first conduct a basic four-pattern with "bounce" (accents). Encourage them to check their posture, make sure their arm is naturally raised, and to conduct down the center of their bodies where the "power supply" (breath) is located.

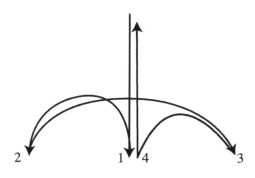

In the first measure, use a percussive "T" consonant to get the breath moving before the pitch. Conduct a four pattern with accents for the first measure, then throw a dart straight forward on beat one of the second measure while singing legato down the scale—keep the eyebrows lifted, breath engaged, and the resonance focused.

Moderately

T T T T Too- ee, oo- ee, oo- ee, oo- ee, oo- ee!__   T T T T Too- ee, oo- ee, oo- ee, oo- ee, oo ee!__

CHAPTER 4:
Finding & Activating Resonance

HOW DO I EXPLAIN RESONANCE IN A WAY MY STUDENTS WILL UNDERSTAND?

Resonance is the projection of the voice as a result of sound waves being amplified inside the hollow spaces in your body. These open spaces are the chest, mouth/throat, and nasal cavities, which are referred to as the "resonators." Resonance is the quality that allows singers to project their voice without apparent effort.

Hard surfaces reflect sound; soft surfaces absorb sound.

The **hard palate** is the "sounding board" of the voice, similar to a sounding board in an acoustic piano.
The hard palate "amplifies" the sound of the vibrating breath coming through the vocal cords. A sounding board in the piano amplifies the sound of the vibrating piano strings.

Ask your singers to take their thumb and place it directly behind their front teeth while raising their eyebrows. Demonstrate the brightest sound possible on "DAH" or "DAE" with the sound focused at the teeth (where the thumb is). Have your students do the same thing. If the paint isn't peeling off the walls in your room, the sound is not truly "at the teeth."

Next, slowly and carefully move the thumb back and feel the hard palate. Demonstrate the sound again, this time focused on the hard palate. The sound is still forward, but now there is more space on the roof of the mouth. Move the thumb back a little further and feel where the hard palate turns into the soft palate. This is now the highest part of the palate, or the "dome" of the mouth.

Demonstrate the sound again and have your students try several times. Try singing a sustained note together while moving the thumb back and forth to mentally focus the sound in different areas of the mouth while keeping their eyebrows raised and jaw dropped.

If you correctly imagine focusing your voice at the hard palate or at the teeth, the two other areas of vibration in the voice (sinus cavities and the chest) vibrate as a result.

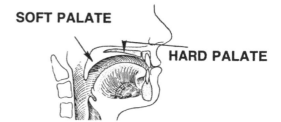

SOFT PALATE

HARD PALATE

WHAT IS THE SCIENCE BEHIND RESONANCE?

The basic scientific definition of resonance is:

The amplification, reinforcement, and prolongation of vibration.

Some basic terminology:

- **SINUS CAVITIES:** There are eight sinus cavities in the front of your face. There are two large ones on either side of your nose, two underneath your eyes, two medium ones between your eyes, and two little ones on either side of your head at your temples. When the sinus cavities are closed, the sound becomes covered or muffled.

- **CHEST CAVITY:** The chest cavity is the chamber of the body that is protected by the thoracic wall (rib cage, muscle, and fascia).

- **PHARYNX:** The part of the throat situated below the mouth and nasal cavity.

- **ORAL CAVITY:** Controls the higher overtones of vowel resonance and musical pitches—the brightness of the voice. The oral cavity does not make the tones, but rather "shapes" and "enhances" them.

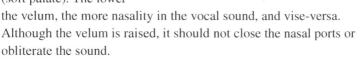

- **NASAL CAVITY:** Controlled by the velum (soft palate). The lower the velum, the more nasality in the vocal sound, and vise-versa. Although the velum is raised, it should not close the nasal ports or obliterate the sound.

- **RING:** a pleasantly vibrant sound that occurs when people sing with a lowered larynx and a high velum (soft palate).

- **TIMBRE:** (pronounced "tam-ber") The tone color or sound quality of a voice. Much like a snowflake, every person's timbre is different and unique to them.

- **SINGER'S FORMANT:** The "buzz" or "ring" in the voice, which occurs in the larynx resonating chamber (small but essential); allows the performer to sing over instruments.

FIVE TIPS FOR CREATING OPTIMUM RESONANCE:

1. Allow your throat to be open with no tension (a lowered larynx—the same sensation as a wide yawn).

2. Raise your soft palate ("yawn").

3. Focus your sound at your hard palate/top front teeth.

4. Relax your lips, jaw, & tongue while raising your eyebrows.

5. Have a "pleasantly surprised," "inner smile" look on your face at all times when singing.

Tip:

Encourage your singers to take private voice lessons with trusted vocal pedagogues. One-on-one instruction is the best way to address the vocal needs of each individual singer. This benefits the entire ensemble, not just the singer.

CHAPTER 5:
Focusing the Resonance

Demonstrate with confidence—your singers will sing EXACTLY how you do.

Use singing vowels (tall, classic, formal British vowels), not speaking vowels (the way we speak on a daily basis) when demonstrating. What's the difference? A raised palate with space for resonance.

If you can speak the proper vowel, you can sing the proper vowel!

FOUR "SUPER RESONANT" VOWELS:

[i] (EE) (as in "Squeeze")

[a] (AH) (as in "Lock")

[e] (AE) (as in "Lay")

[æ] (Aa) (as in "Dad")

SPIRITC

- **FOCUSED HUM -** Ask the singers to massage their cheekbones while humming with an "inner smile." Focus the sound at the teeth with an "Ee" vowel hum (practice humming with a different vowel shape inside the mouth).

Slowly *molto legato*

Mm_____   Mm_____

- **MUSTACHE** - Make sure the previous exercise begins with a "puff of air" out the nose so that the breath begins before the sound. Do the exercise again and have your students make a "mustache" and feel the gentle puff of air at the start of each phrase.

Tip:

When the exercise gets too low, encourage the Tenor voices to sing up the octave where it is more comfortable for them.

- **ICE CREAM** - While pretending to eat a bowl of your favorite ice cream, sing "Yum, Yum, Yum, Yum, Yum!" Brighten the tone as you go down the scale.

Yum Yum Yum Yum Yum!   Yum Yum Yum Yum Yum!

Ask the singers what kind of ice cream is their favorite, have them share with one another, then have them look around at each other while eating (singing)...

- **WINDSHIELD WIPERS -** Try the same "ice cream" exercise on "Yai yai yai yai yai." This time move windshield wipers in front of your eyes with your index finger. The sound should be even brighter than when eating the ice cream!

- **DANCE PARTY -** Sing "Vee, Vee, Vee" or "Fee, Fee, Fee" with staccato articulation. Extend your right hand out in front of body, eyebrows up, chin down. Make a tall karate chop vertically with each sung pitch. Once the singers get the hang of it, have a dance party by moving the body from side to side while singing, moving to the left first. Remember to ask for tall posture and a resonant, forward tone on every note. Sing the "Ee" vowel through "Oo" lips to create optimum space.

Moderately

	Vee	Vee	Vee		Vee	Vee	Vee
	Fee	Fee	Fee		Fee	Fee	Fee

- **JACKHAMMER/CONFETTI** - Sing up the scale on "Dee, Doo, Yo ho ho!" Both arms out front, as if holding on to a steering wheel. For each ascending staccato note, move arms in a "jackhammer" motion, then toss an arm up on the first "Yo." Tell the singers to release all energy on that note, along with a handful of imaginary confetti! When moving through the passagio, change "Yo" to "Yah" to open the vowel. Drop the jaw and allow for more resonant space.

Confetti

Jackhammer

- **DARK TO BRIGHT** - Sing a unison A♭ for eight counts on an "Ah." Have the singers sing from the darkest vowel to the brightest vowel possible. Try on different vowels to play with tone color.

- **BRO BOUNCE** – Extend an arm in front of body, elbow bent, with hand parallel to the torso. Drop the jaw and sing "Yoh ho ho ho ho" or ("Bro ho ho ho ho", flipping the "R") with staccato articulation. Keep the arm straight and gently "bounce arm" on the four major beats in each measure. As the notes get higher, modify the vowel to "Yah" to allow for more space in the mouth. Keep eyes alert with eyebrows up.

Moderately

Bro ho ho ho ho,
Yah ha ha ha ha,

Bro ho ho ho ho,
Yah ha ha ha ha,

Tip:

Constantly remind your singers: When in doubt, sing "AH!" When we go to the doctor there is a reason why he/she asks us to stick out our tongue and say "AH"—this is the vowel that creates the most space inside the entire mouth.

- **FRISBEE TIME -** Now try the same exercise, but legato this time. Release a Frisbee on the high note, let the sound and body be free, and find the "ring" while letting the Frisbee soar in the air. Prep to throw the Frisbee when taking a low, deep breath on beat four. Explain what a prep beat is, and its importance, and have them conduct a simple four pattern with a prep beat.

Yoh_____
Yah_____

Yoh_____
Yah_____

- **MAKE IT RAIN -** Become an instant billionaire and share your wealth with one another while singing by holding your hands out flat in front of you— one palm up, the other palm down. Make a smooth motion on each beat that indicates cash flying around! Keep the sound light and bright and focused at the hard palate.

Moderately

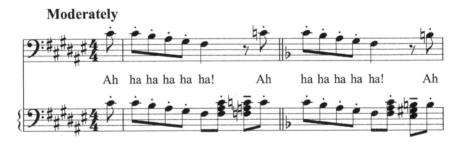

Ah ha ha ha ha ha! Ah ha ha ha ha ha! Ah

- **ITALIAN DINNER** - Using your hands, body, and facial expressions, bounce on a single pitch while singing this exercise. Focus on shadow vowels. Remind your singers that the Italian language is a Romance language that involves a lot of energy, passion, and intensity. The sound is made with the lips, tip of the tongue, and teeth! Breathe IN the first vowel (AH) and move around the room.

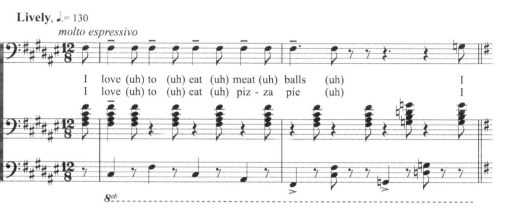

Lively, ♩.= 130
molto espressivo

I love (uh) to (uh) eat (uh) meat (uh) balls (uh) I
I love (uh) to (uh) eat (uh) piz - za pie (uh) I

CHAPTER 6:
Tuning the Resonance

Around the sixth month of my first year of teaching middle and high school guys I remember a rehearsal where every sound the guys made was just plain LOUD. I thought to myself, "what have I done?!" Once young men find their full, resonant voice, it is definitely a challenge to get them to "pull back" and to tune their sound. But it IS possible with persistence and perseverance. It truly is a great problem to have! You can always ask for less sound, but you won't know what their full potential sound is until you've asked for everything they've got.

How can we maintain the resonance but control the overall volume of the ensemble?

- Continue to ask for an energized, resonant, and focused tone on a daily basis.
- Allow for freedom and flexibility in the sound, and make adjustments in dynamics as needed.
- Encourage your students to sing THROUGH each vowel and phrase with forward momentum.
- Remind your students to sing with an open, relaxed throat.
- Spend time working on resonance every day. Incorporate resonant singing throughout your entire rehearsal—not just in the warm-ups.

- **VOWEL FOCUS** – Sing "Vee, Ae, Eh, Ah" on a D major chord progression. Practice focusing the sound.

Have your singers make a unicorn horn and extend their arm while singing this exercise to help "focus" the sound. Pick a point on the wall and tell them to direct their sound to that specific point.

Ask your singers to try this exercise a number of different ways:
- Sing like untrained fourth graders
- Sing like average middle school students
- Sing like a mediocre high school choir, then a stellar high school choir
- Sing like a college senior who is taking voice lessons
- Be a collegiate men's ensemble
- Be a Broadway star
- Be an opera singer
- Be a professional choral ensemble—you are now getting paid to sing!!

Then ask them "What did you change? What sounded different?" "What should our choir "sound" like? "Are we being true to ourselves and to our own sound?"

Next, make a "Quadricorn" and ask for four times the amount of energy and resonance! If the sound is woofy or covered, ask your students to "show their fangs" – didn't you know that quadricorns have fangs and like to show them off?!

It's All In the Vowels

Encourage your students to sing with their full voice and full self at all times. Blending is in the vowel – not in the volume – of each individual singer. **Dynamics are relative!** Remember that the score is simply a guide. A "mp" marking for a choir of 200 adult singers is not going to sound the same as a "mp" marking for a choir of twenty young men. Take the dynamic markings with a grain of salt. You have to find a true fortissimo for each ensemble before you can begin to pull back and find what that ensemble's true "mp" really is. Don't be afraid to make changes in the score to fit the needs of your choir.

I often hear teachers say, "My guys can't sing in tune!" My response is, "Yes they can. It's all in the vowels." Have two of your best singers come to the front of the room. Ask one to sing the proper vowel and the other to sing a lazy version of the same vowel. Then ask that singer to listen and adjust. Show your excitement when the vowels are the same (aligned and in tune). Ask the class if they heard it, then do it again. Have more guys come up and demonstrate, and then practice it with each section of the choir.

> **Tip:**
> Number your singers off by twos. Have the number ones sing a phrase or exercise while the number twos close their eyes and listen, and vice versa. Ask the students to give feedback. What did they hear?

- **ENSEMBLE RESONANCE** - Using an E♭ Major chord (or transpose to a more comfortable key for your singers), begin on a mezzo-piano "Noo" (warm, rich, yet resonant). Descend by half steps while listening for pure intonation among the ensemble. They should descend in this order: T2, T1/T2, ALL, B1/B2, B1/B2, T1 to resolve to C Major chord (see below). Try this with various dynamics and vowels ("mf" Noh, "f" Nah, "p" Nee, etc.). Remember to modify the vowel on higher notes—when in doubt, drop your jaw and sing "Ah!"

Remind your singers to listen louder than they sing and to keep the breath spinning (stir that pot of spaghetti).

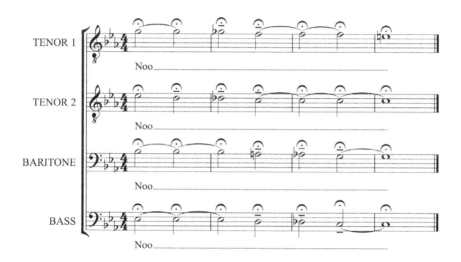

If one note out of five is out of tune, the vowel preceding the problem note is usually where the true "problem" lies. Have the singers stop and hold that vowel and adjust to tune (the same as if they were playing a wind or string instrument). It is important to remember that it is our job to help singers develop their "ears" (listening skills) as well as their voices. They must be able to actively listen and reflect on what they are hearing at all times during rehearsal.

> **Tip:**
> Constantly encourage your singers to sing with "internal" energy. They should be able to feel the energy from their hair to their toes at all times.

CHAPTER 7:
Repertoire & Rehearsal Ideas

Don't settle for the sea shanty!

REPERTOIRE

An ensemble's success is almost entirely determined by the quality and appropriateness of their repertoire. It is extremely important to spend time finding the correct repertoire for each and every ensemble. Don't treat your guys like the stereotypical "boy's choir." It is not fair to them, to you, or to your audience. Young men are fully capable of singing high quality literature in all styles.

SA can be TB in most cases. SATB can be TTBB in most cases:

- Tenor 1 sing Alto line, as written
- Tenor 2 sing Soprano line 1 octave lower
- Baritone sing Tenor line, as written
- Bass sing Bass line, as written

Try a variety of voicings that fit the needs of your ensemble: unison/TB/TTB/TBB/TTBB, etc. If you have eight novice singers in your choir, try not to program TTBB music, as they will most likely be much more successful singing TB repertoire. Again, look at the needs of each ensemble and choose repertoire that will challenge them, but that you are certain they will ultimately be able to perform successfully.

Young men need to sing repertoire with historical and musical significance. They need music they can relate to with texts that have depth and truth in them. These are pieces with meaningful words that they don't get to say out loud anywhere else. I have listed a wealth of repertoire suggestions in the Appendix that fit this description.

REHEARSAL IDEAS

- Know exactly what you want each piece of music to sound and look like before you begin rehearsing. The rehearsal focus should be on pulling the sound and life out of the music, not on the details in the printed music itself.

- Don't stand behind the music stand all the time when rehearsing. If you don't know the music by memory, grab the score and move around. Have the guys stand in circles in sections or small groups. They love to "huddle" like a football team and they can hear each other better.

- Constantly remind your singers to hold their music high. The body must be fully expanded and music should be held at neck level so you can see their eyes at all times.

- Use staccato "doot" and "dah" to rehearse any piece of music. These are powerful tools to help articulate sound and focus pitch on every note.

- If singers are having a difficult time singing an ascending phrase in their upper register, ask them to "put their best foot forward" (in a lunge position). Sing the line again, but this time as the line ascends tell the singers to put all of their weight and momentum on their leg that is extended in the lunge position. The age-old saying applies: **"sing high, think low."** This ensures that the singers are "grounded."

- Having a hard time focusing? Put up your blinders! In Kansas City, around the holidays, there are horse-drawn carriages that take people for rides around the plaza to enjoy the lights and sights. These horses have on "blinders," which cause them to focus on one thing only: moving forward! Ask your singers to put up their horse blinders and focus their sound and energy forward.

- Keep in mind that your singers will perform how they practice, so they should practice how you think they should perform, every second of every rehearsal. Ask questions of your singers frequently— ninety percent of the time they know exactly why you stopped to fix something. Make eye contact, smile, and be energetic!

- Get rid of all the "RRR'S" in the score. They get in the way of pure vowels and young men struggle with this. Simply cross them out and replace with a "schwa." Write out the IPA and explain that it is a neutral vowel. [ə]

- Designate time for "good news" during rehearsals. Ask students to raise their hands and share good things that are happening in their lives.

FAILING IS A MUST!

The great Walt Disney once said:

"I think it's important to have a good hard failure when you're young. I learned a lot out of that. It makes you kind of aware of what can happen to you. Because of it I've never been afraid."

In my opinion, this quote directly applies to rehearsals and to making music. Don't be afraid to let your singers know when they have failed and when something doesn't sound good. It's not being negative, it's being realistic, and it makes them stronger and more aware. When something amazing really does happen, you will light up and so will the singers. If we don't fail, we don't learn. Encourage your singers to continue singing after they make a mistake. Make the mistake, learn from it (circle it), then move on.

- We are not just teaching children how to sing. We are teaching them important life lessons every day in our rehearsals. Teach your singers how to iron their shirts and pants for performances. Show them how to tie a tie. Explain why it is important.

- Encourage your young men to "own the stage." When it comes time for a performance, walk quickly on and off risers, smiling, with a purpose! Practice getting on and off stage while smiling days before the performance (it doesn't just happen). Every detail of a performance must be thoroughly planned out, well practiced, and executed.

- If you have your male singers in a room without girls, talk with them about puberty, and that the voice crack is normal. The "hole" (missing pitches) in their voice is normal during the voice change. Remind them that the more they work through that strange "break," the easier it will become to sing.

Conclusion

Hopefully, after reading this book, you are now thinking to yourself "I can do this." Yes, you can! It is, however, important to remember that what works for one person might not work for the next. Again, take what works for you and your choir and leave out what does not. As you experiment with the various exercises and ideas provided, be aware that most young men respond well to honesty, tough love, and laughter. It is a lot to think about when we are focused on the music and the high expectations we have set for our students, but we should try to include these elements in every rehearsal. Allow your natural musical instincts to serve as your guide, and make adjustments and changes appropriately and efficiently. Enjoy the journey!

Appendix:
Suggested Repertoire

TB

TITLE	COMPOSER/ ARRANGER	PUBLISHER
Lasst uns mit geschlungnen Handn	W.A. Mozart	EC Schirmer
O du Eselhafter Martin (canon)	W.A. Mozart	EC Schirmer
Kyrie Eleison	Dan Davison	Walton Music
Laudate Dominum	Dan Davison	Walton Music
Regina Coeli	Dan Davison	Walton Music
Gloria	Dan Davison	Walton Music
Yellow Bird	arr. Dan Davison	Walton Music
A La Nanita Nana	arr. Dan Davison	Walton Music
The Coventry Carol	arr. Mark Patterson	BriLee Music
Battle Cry of Freedom	arr. Jason Cole	Santa Barbara
Santa Lucia	Cottrau/ed. Leck	Hal Leonard
American Folk Rhapsody	Linda Spevacek	Heritage Music
Down in the Valley	arr. D. Shawn Berry	Santa Barbara
Ev'ry Night When the Sun...	arr. D. Shawn Berry	Santa Barbara
Hine Ma Tov	arr. Neil Ginsberg	Santa Barbara
If You've Only Got a Moustache	arr. Stephen Rotz	Santa Barbara
Kansas City Kitty	arr. Jacob Narverud	Santa Barbara
Zion Hears the Watchmen Singing	Deitrich Buxtehude	EC Schirmer
Zum Gali Gali	arr. Greg Gilpin	Heritage Music
Jubilate Deo	Mozart/arr. Spevacek	Heritage Music
De' Animals A-Comin' (also TTBB)	arr. Bartholomew	G. Schirmer
Gone, Gone, Gone	arr. Andy Beck	Alfred Music
May God Bless You (Der Herr Segne Euch)	J.S. Bach/arr. Talley	Hal Leonard

TTB

TITLE	COMPOSER/ ARRANGER	PUBLISHER
O Burning Mountain	Neil Ginsberg	Santa Barbara
Cover Me with the Night	Andrea Ramsey	Alliance Music
Home on the Range	arr. Andrea Ramsey	Hal Leonard
Hallelujah for the Day!	Andrea Ramsey	Hal Leonard
Workin' on the Railroad	Donald Moore	Alfred Music
Byker Hill	Mitchell Sandler	Hinshaw Music
Armonia	Dan Davison	Walton Music
Who Are The Brave?	Joseph M. Martin	Alfred Music
Colorado Trail	arr. Donald Moore	BriLee Music
Spirituals Medley	arr. Lon Beery	BriLee Music
Star of the County Down	arr. Douglas E. Wagner	Alfred Music
Come, Ye Sons of Art	Purcell/Land	Plymouth Music
This Train	arr. Roger Emerson	Hal Leonard
Tell My Father	arr. Andrea Ramsey	Hal Leonard
Come, Holy Spirit	Mozart/arr. DeCesare	Exsultet Music
Laudate Dominum	Mozart/arr. Johns	Alfred Music
Ani Ma'amin	arr. John Leavitt	Hal Leonard
Hine Ma Tov	arr. Lon Beery	Shawnee Press
Festival Sanctus	John Leavitt	Alfred Music
Polly Wolly Doddle	arr. John Leavitt	Hal Leonard
Old Dan Tucker	arr. John Leavitt	Hal Leonard

TBB

TITLE	COMPOSER/ ARRANGER	PUBLISHER
'O Sole Mio	arr. Jacob Narverud	Santa Barbara
Men in Tights	Brooks/arr. Narverud	Shawnee Press
Dominus Vobiscum	Jacob Narverud	Carl Fischer
Jambo	Harrison/arr. Narverud	Santa Barbara
Stitches	arr. Narverud	Shawnee Press
Dust in the Wind	Livgren/arr. Narverud	Shawnee Press
Learning to Love Again	Kearney/arr. Narverud	Hal Leonard

TBB (continued)

TITLE	COMPOSER/ ARRANGER	PUBLISHER
Amor Vittorioso	Gastoldi/ed. Leininger	Alliance Music
The Auctioneer	arr. Kirby Shaw	Hal Leonard
Homeward Bound	Keen/arr. Althouse	Alfred Music
God Rest You Merry, Gentlemen	arr. Tucker Courtney	BriLee Music
Two Renaissance Chorals	Palestrina/Archadelt/ Robinson	Alfred Music
Nine Hundred Miles	Philip E. Silvey	Santa Barbara
Stopping by Woods on a Snowy...	Randall Thompson	EC Schirmer
Ich Liebe Dich	Beethoven/arr. Larkin	Alliance Music
Alleluia	Bach/Lefebvre	EC Schirmer
I've Got Peace Like a River	arr. D. Shawn Berry	Santa Barbara
Comin' Thro the Rye	arr. Ashley Nelson	Santa Barbara
My Heart's In the Highlands	Donald Moore	Alfred Music
Adoramus Te Christe	Lassus/Weinrich	Golden Music

TTBB

TITLE	COMPOSER/ ARRANGER	PUBLISHER
'Gloria' from the Twelfth Mass	Mozart/Mueller/ arr. Narverud	Santa Barbara
Pompeii	Smith/arr. Narverud	Shawnee Press
Quest of the Kings	arr. Narverud	Santa Barbara
Demon in my View	Jeffrey T. Horvath	Alfred Music
Zion's Walls	Copland/arr. Koponen	Hal Leonard
Noel	Smith/arr. Holmes	First Step
Dirait-on	Morten Lauridsen	Peer Music
The Ground	Ola Gjeilo	Walton Music
Salmo 150	Ernani Aguiar	Earthsongs
Et In Terra Pax	Vivaldi/arr. Martens	Walton Music
At the Round Earth's Imagined...	Rene Clausen	Santa Barbara
Pirate Song	Tim Y. Jones	Alliance Music

TTBB (continued)

TITLE	COMPOSER/ ARRANGER	PUBLISHER
Bonse Aba	arr. Andrew Fischer	Alliance Music
Ubi Caritas	Ola Gjeilo	Walton Music
Workin' on the Railroad	arr. Terry J. Barham	Santa Barbara
Three Graduals	Czerny/ed. Banner	Colla Voce
Sometimes I Feel	arr. Alice Parker	Alfred Music
Gaudete!	arr. Michael Engelhardt	Walton Music
Come Sing to Me of Heaven	arr. J. Aaron McDermid	Mark Foster
The Last Words of David	Randall Thompson	EC Schirmer
Kansas City Jones	Jackson Berkey	SDG Press
Song of Peace	Vincent Persichetti	Theodore Presser
Idumea	arr. Richard Bjella	Alliance Music
Tshotsholoza	Jeffrey L. Ames	Walton Music
My Soul's Been Anchored in the Lord	arr. Hogan/ed. Eklund	Hal Leonard
Jagerchor (Huntsmen's Chorus)	Carl Maria von Weber	Schott Music
O Sing to the Lord	Dan Davison	Walton Music
Cantate Domino	Hassler/ed.Taylor	Alliance Music
And So It Goes	Joel/arr. Shaw	Hal Leonard
Prayer of the Children	Bestor/arr. Klouse	Alfred Music
Brothers, Sing On	Grieg/ed. McKinney	Alfred Music
Vive L'Amour	arr. Terry J. Barham	Santa Barbara
Four Folk Songs for Male Voices	arr. Dale Grotenhuis	National Music
We Shall Walk Through the Valley	William Appling	World Library
Du bist die Ruh	Schubert/arr. Eklund	Santa Barbara
Fergus an' Molly	Vijay Singh	Alfred Music
Joshua Fit de Battle of Jericho	arr. Howard Helvey	Beckenhorst
The Music of Living	Dan Forrest	Hinshaw Music
The Awakening	Joseph M. Martin	Shawnee Press
Do You Fear the Wind?	Leland B. Sateren	Alfred Music
I See the Heaven's Glories Shine	Andrea Ramsey	Santa Barbara
Riders in the Sky	Jones/arr. Luboff	Hal Leonard
Poor Lonesome Cowboy	arr. Luboff	Walton Music

TTBB (continued)

TITLE	COMPOSER/ ARRANGER	PUBLISHER
The Roof	Andrea Ramsey	Hal Leonard
Bound for Jubilee	Joyce Eilers	Alfred Music
Hark, I Hear the Harps Eternal	arr. Alice Parker	Alfred Music
Things that Never Die	Lee Dengler	Shawnee Press
Swingin' with the Saints	arr. Mark Hayes	Shawnee Press
Cool Water	Nolan/Ringwald	Shawnee Press
Mary Sat A-Rockin'	Greg Gilpin	Shawnee Press
Cindy	arr. Alice Parker	Santa Barbara
It Takes a Village	Joan Szymko	Santa Barbara
Barcarolle	Offenbach/arr. Dudley	Santa Barbara
Two Folk Songs for Male Voices	John Rutter	Oxford Press
Beati Mortui	Mendelssohn/ed. Weber	Alliance Music
'Sanctus' (Holy Is the Lord)	Schubert/arr. Davis	Colla Voce
Vive L'Amour	arr. Shaw/Parker	Alfred Music
'Sicut locutus est' from Magnificat	J.S. Bach/arr. Mishkin	EC Schirmer
'Dies Irae' from Requiem	Mozart/arr. Liebergen	Alfred Music
Alleluia	Randall Thompson	EC Schirmer
Ose Shalom	John Leavitt	Hal Leonard
'Gloria' from Gloria	Vivaldi/arr. Leavitt	Hal Leonard
We Sail the Ocean Blue	Gilbert & Sullivan/ arr. Leavitt	Hal Leonard
Muddy Water	arr. John Leavitt	Hal Leonard
Dry Bones	arr. Mark Hayes	Alfred Music
De Profundis	Arvo Part	Universal Edition
Bright Morning Stars	Shawn Kirchner	Santa Barbara
Brightest and Best	Shawn Kirchner	Boosey & Hawkes

About the Author

Jacob Narverud is an active composer, arranger, conductor, and clinician. He is the Composer-In-Residence with the Allegro Choirs of Kansas City, where he conducts 'Spirito' Young Men's Ensemble and 'Brillante' Chamber Choir. A native of Meriden, Kansas, Narverud earned degrees from the Conservatory of Music at the University of Missouri-Kansas City (MM Conducting), where he studied with Robert Bode and also founded 'Amphion' Men's Ensemble, and Emporia State University (BM Vocal Performance/Education), where he studied with Terry Barham. Jake has taught at both secondary and collegiate levels, as Associate Director of Choirs at Lawrence Free State High School and as Interim Director of Choral Activities at Emporia State University. Narverud has performed with the Kansas City Chorale and the Kansas City Symphony as a back-up singer for Ben Folds. He has prepared choruses for conductors Michael Stern, Jack Everly, Anthony Edwards, and Charles Bruffy. Professional memberships include ACDA, ASCAP, NCCO, NATS, and Chorus America. Narverud's music is published by Wingert-Jones, Santa Barbara, Alliance, Carl Fischer, G. Schirmer, Alfred, Shawnee Press, and Hal Leonard.

'SPIRITO' Young Men's Ensemble Allegro Choirs of Kansas City

Since its creation in 1999, Allegro has grown from one youth choir of thirty-eight singers to over 250 singers in six ensembles. Today, our singers represent students in the third through twelfth grades. Drawn from across the Kansas City metro area, these talented young singers come from private, public and home-school environments. Allegro Choirs delight audience members each year – locally, nationally, and abroad – with their varied repertoire and heartfelt singing. Allegro con Spirito (est. 2012) is an ensemble for young men with changing and changed voices. Rehearsals are fast-paced with a focus on vocal development and musicianship skills. The young men of Spirito pride themselves on being a brotherhood of first- rate showmen and positive role models in the community. Spirito served as the choir-in-residence at Vandercook College of Music in Chicago in 2013 and was invited to sing at the Kansas Music Educator's Association Convention in 2014, Colorado in 2015, and the Southwest American Choral Director's Association convention in 2016. Spirito will tour Italy in the summer of 2016. Learn more at www.allegrokc.org